Your Credit Score DeBugged

Peter Emm

Copyright © 2019 Peter Emm

All rights reserved.

This book is solely aimed at enlightening the reader/buyer about the covered subject. It is not legal, psychological, financial or other professional advice and therefore, the author and the publisher are not liable for its application.

The author uses the name "Ken" fictitiously to explain concepts and therefore, any resemblance to any person is a coincidence.

YourCreditScoreDeBugged@gmail.com

First Edition

ISBN: 978-1734104318

Acknowledgments

This book would not have been written without the help of the following:

The Almighty God, for His constant, unparalleled inspiration.

Abby and Ayda, for giving me a quiet atmosphere to work.

My wife Naomi, for her encouragement and advice.

Lynn Bosworth, for editing every page in this book.

Angie Alaya, for her advice and creative-artful cover design.

Julia Bramer, for her advice and tireless formatting of this book.

I'm also thankful to everybody else that encouraged or assisted me because, without them, this book would have remained a dream.

Contents

Introduction

Your credit score is a tool like any other. Some people like myself (at one point) ignore their credit score, and they have no idea how much money they can save if they paid a little attention to their credit rating. That is why I wrote this book; to enlighten anybody out there who might have a poor credit score or credit score that is not where it is supposed to be. Once you know why your credit score is bad, I do not doubt that you would want to make it better. Once your credit is good or excellent, it will open doors that you have never imagined. You will save money. You will improve your wealth.

1··Poor Credit Score

Three years ago, my credit score was poor. Within the next three years, one major thing happened — my eyes flew wide open, which made me view my credit score in a way that I had never done before. I became aware of my financial/credit management mistakes and made a conscious decision to take corrective action. With that remedial action, my credit score improved from poor to excellent.

To give you an idea about my credit score's slow crawl to where it is today, in March this year, I had a credit score of 780 based on VantageScore 3.0. Today, the first of August, I have a credit score of 814. Within five months, my credit score improved by 34 points. It has been a slow and arduous process, but it has happened. That is why I'm excited to tell you about this journey.

2··How Did I Get There?

Before I explain how I got there, you need to know that I had two types of debt. The first was a college loan that amounted to $50,000, which I accumulated ten years ago while pursuing a second degree.

The second type was credit card debt. I had two credit cards that had an approximate balance of $6,000 and zero usable credit. Every month, this credit card company sent me bills with minimum payments that totaled a little over $200. I paid these minimum payments without much thought or care about what they meant.

3··The Turning Point

One night, I was shredding my credit card bills, and I calculated the total amount of interest that the cards had charged me. I could not believe my eyes! In the first quarter of 2016, my two credit cards had charged me $345. I was paying through the nose for my credit card debt. The credit card bills also indicated that if I continued making minimum payments, which I often did, I could end up paying my credit card debt for years to come. To make matters worse, I would pay thousands of dollars in interest fees! That was insane! From that moment on, I decided to avoid making minimum payments whenever I could. I also decided to work as hard as I could to clear my credit balances as soon as possible.

To achieve my goal, I planned to get extra money from wherever I could. I worked overtime and tried to cut my expenses to the bare minimum. I avoided my expensive leisure activities such as going to bars, casinos, and even going out for movies. I reduced the number of times I took my family out for dinner. I also cut my family shopping lists to just what we needed. That way, I was able to save a lot of my money. Within three years, I had zero credit card balance!

4··Why Write This Book?

The answer is straightforward: to help people out there who have poor FICO scores. FICO score improvement is personal to me because I have had both poor and excellent credit scores. I have known firsthand the pain and embarrassment of a poor FICO score. Yet, I have also reaped the benefits of an excellent credit score. I don't want anybody else to experience the difficulties I endured, but I would love every reader to enjoy the freedom that excellent credit scores afford.

I don't want to create an impression that anyone who reads this book will improve their FICO credit score in one week or a month because that did not happen to me. Instead, I intend to equip my readers with information which might slowly and steadily improve their FICO credit scores. Rome was not built in a day, and I believe that still holds in our FICO score improvement effort! I have taken many baby steps in the last three years to pay thousands of dollars in credit card debt. Those little steps have led me almost to the peak of the FICO credit scores mountain. It is my hope that sharing my experience might help some of my readers to figure out ways to improve their FICO score.

5··What Is a FICO Score?

Let's assume Ken wants to borrow $100 from you. How will you know that he will pay you back? For you to lend him the money, it is crucial to know the risk involved. Otherwise, you may be hesitant to help him. But if Ken had borrowed money from you many times before and paid it back, you can assume that it is safe to lend it to him again. If you were to rate Ken's credit worthiness, what score, as a percentage, would you give him? Probably close to 100%.

Just as we have painted Ken's credit worthiness in percentage terms, the credit score does the same thing for lending institutions, although in a much more complicated way. Lenders have used FICO scores in the United States since the late 1980s. A FICO score uses one's credit history, payment history, age of the latest line of credit, and what I will call *credit mix* in its calculations. To improve your FICO score, you need to know the importance of these factors. We will look at these factors more closely in a little bit.

6··Types of FICO Scores

Different types of FICO scores tell lenders about our credit risk. It is crucial for you to know that lending institutions have not come to a consensus on a single credit rating system for them all to use, but just as the computer algorithms for analyzing data have evolved, the FICO scores have changed, too. That means that the system to determine FICO scores has been improved many times since they were first used in the U.S. The latest credit rating system is FICO 9, and before that, there was FICO 8. Even though both measure credit risk, they don't emphasize the same things. For example, if a consumer pays one of his monthly payments late but the previous 60 were paid on time, one FICO score might penalize him while the other might overlook it.

In addition, some institutions of lending are not satisfied with a base FICO score, and therefore, they have had them fine-tuned to be in sync with their business needs. For instance, a bank might use FICO *bankcard* score 5, 8, or 9 while a car dealership might use FICO *auto* score 5, 8 or 9, respectively. Furthermore, institutions of lending might not adopt a new FICO score at the same time. It is common knowledge that if one requests his or her FICO score from the three credit bureaus (Experian, TransUnion, and Equifax) at the same time, he or she might get different scores. How can that be the case if credit reporting agencies are dealing with the same person? One reason is that the three agencies might not have the same information about a person, or the agencies use different FICO score algorithms in their calculations.

7··How Do You Know if Your Credit Score Is Poor or Excellent?

Most people in the U.S. have credit scores that range from 300 to 850. If Ken's credit score is 800 and above, he is considered to have excellent credit rating. If he mismanages his debt payment and his credit score hovers anywhere between 740 and 799, his credit score is said to be very good. If his credit score continues to deteriorate and one day he wakes up to find it hovering between 670 and 739, then his credit score is good. If his credit score continues to get worse and it settles between 580 and 669, his credit rating is said to be fair. If his credit falls below that range (i.e., below 580), his credit score is poor.

There are other classifications of credit scores, but the critical thing to know is where your score lies; if it is not good and above or where you want it to be, probably you need to improve it.

8··Why Is Your FICO Score Important?

Your FICO score is important to you because it is invaluable to institutions of lending for three reasons:

1. It helps lenders to decide whether or not to lend you their money. If you are a risky customer, I do not need to tell you what their decision will be!

2. It assists lenders to decide your rate of interest You pay a higher interest rate if your credit score is poor and vice versa.

3. Lending institutions use it to determine the amount of down payment their customer pays when he or she is buying a car, for example.

From this, we can draw two conclusions:

1. Your FICO score determines how lending institutions treat your loan application.

2. Your FICO score can impact the amount of money you have.

The million-dollar question: How does Ken quickly improve his credit rating if he finds himself with a poor credit rating?

One evening at the time when my credit rating was abysmal, I visited a local bank and asked the manager to lend me a thousand dollars. "Let me see if we can do that," the manager said, as she typed my information into her computer. Suddenly, she stopped typing, looked me in the eye, and asked, "What do you need the money for?"

"To fund my business," I answered.

She typed some more on her computer, and after five tense minutes, she sat up, folded her bare arms across her chest, and looked at me with a solemn face. Before she could say a word, I knew my financial coffin was sealed, and there was no way to escape.

"We are not going to do that," she said.

"Why?" I asked.

"Several reasons," she continued. "First, several of your credit accounts are maxed; second, you have recently been taken to a collection agency for non-payment of a debt; and lastly, your debt-to-credit ratio is in terrible shape."

With shoulders hunched, I walked out of the bank, empty-handed. Knowing what my credit report/credit score did to me that sad evening, I am motivated to share my experience with you, my readers, because it might open your eyes to the fact that life does not have to be as bleak as mine was that evening.

9··Options Available to Ken

There are options available to Ken, depending on his situation. I will discuss each one of these situations and then suggest solutions that might help him.

The first thing that Ken should do is to get his credit report. He can get a free credit report at annualcreditreport.com. Once he has a copy of this report, he will be able to see if there is any information that adversely affects his credit rating. Some adverse information can impact his credit rating for up to 10 years, depending on the nature of the data. For instance, a collection agency might have reported to the credit reporting agency that it had intervened on behalf of another company when Ken failed to honor his debt obligations. The report also indicates if or when Ken had been arrested or imprisoned for a felony.

10··How Does Adverse Information on the Credit Report Impact Ken?

Lenders, such as banks and auto-dealers, transact business every day with thousands of people. To make decisions about whom to extend their credit services to, lending institutions turn to credit reports. The information on the credit reports tell lenders how risky their potential customer might be. If the credit report indicates that Ken does not pay his debt obligations on time, has filed for bankruptcy, or has been in jail on felony charges, the lender might decide not to transact business with him because Ken might be too risky.

If for any reason a lending institution decides to allow Ken to borrow some money, he might have to pay a higher interest rate than another person who does not have similar adverse information in his or her credit report. Employers might decide not to hire Ken if his credit report has information that adversely impacts his credit. For example, if Ken has filed for bankruptcy, an employer might think that Ken would not make a great financial manager; therefore, Ken might not get his dream job.

Negative information on Ken's credit report might impact his ability to rent an apartment. If a potential landlord discovers that Ken's credit history is littered with bankruptcy filings, late debt payments, and debt collection alerts, the landlord might think that history would repeat itself if he rented Ken an apartment.

11·· What is Ken Supposed to Do with Adverse Information on His Credit Report?

If such information is an error and he can prove that is the case, he should contact the credit reporting agencies, lending institutions, and collection agencies involved so that such information is removed from his credit report. If adverse information on Ken's credit report is accurate, Ken has only one option. He has to try to clear the adverse information himself. He should pay the collection agencies or lending institutions that took him to the debt collectors.

If he is behind in paying any of his debts, he has to do a better job. He has to know that he can't afford to be behind in his payments anymore! If he has done everything he can in the right way, then all he needs to do is to be patient because adverse information becomes less impactful over time and will eventually "drop out" of his credit report.

In 2016, I took my sick child to a local hospital. After my child was treated, the hospital staff told me that the billing department would prepare my bill and then send it to me in the next couple of days. I never got the bill. Was it my problem? I didn't think so. One day, about six weeks later, I received a phone call from a lady who claimed to be a collection agent. She told me that I had failed to pay my debt obligation after visiting a local hospital. I knew I was in trouble. I asked for her information so that I could call her back after talking to the hospital. In minutes, I was on another call to hospital, trying to find out why it had taken me to a debt collection agency. The hospital claimed that its staff couldn't find my contact information and therefore wasn't able to send me the bill. That was bullshit because I had dealt with the hospital for years, and the hospital had billed me many times for its services.

I asked to speak to the manager who admitted that his staff had made an error when they took me to the collection agency. I paid the manager for my child's treatment and requested him to authorize the collection agency to stop collecting on the hospital's behalf because a collection error had been made from the beginning. A few months later, the collection alert which had adversely affected my credit rating disappeared from my credit report.

12··Is Obtaining a Credit Report All Ken Needs?

The answer is *no*. A credit report on its own does not paint a complete picture of Ken's credit worthiness, and therefore, he would have to obtain his FICO credit score. To obtain his FICO credit score, Ken can either buy it from a credit reporting agency or, if possible, get it for free from his credit card provider.

13··How Is the FICO Credit Score Calculated?

Ken should know how his FICO credit score is determined because different factors are given different weights during that calculation process. These factors include:

Payment history

Ken's payment history tells us whether he pays his debts on time. Paying debts on time is the single most critical factor in determining Ken's FICO credit score. If Ken does not pay his bills on time every month, his credit rating takes a big hit. Late payment or non-payment of debt remains in his credit report for many years. Lenders who might want to do business with Ken pay particular interest to his payment history. They need to know whether he will pay them on time or not. His payment history determines about 35% of his FICO credit score. If he pays his debts on time and fulfills all other requirements, then his FICO credit score should be excellent.

Three years ago, I didn't pay much attention to due dates on my bills, and saying that it was a big mistake is an understatement. I cannot say why I was delinquent on bill payment, but I guess I was careless, lazy, or both. Many times, I received text messages from different lenders informing me that I was late paying my bills. Some lenders even called me, which shows how bad my situation was. I remember one morning, around 8:30, I was at a busy intersection waiting for a green light when a caller with area code 800 called. I did not know the caller, so I ignored the call but listened to the voicemail just before the lights turned green. The bank that owned my two maxed-out credit cards had called and needed to know why I was consistently late in my payments. The bank also wanted to find out if I needed any money-management advice. As I said earlier, I woke up from my financial slumber when I calculated the amount of interest I was paying for my credit card debt. I realized that paying high-interest rates for my credit card debt together with late payment fees was not only sucking resources meant for my family, but it was also slowly ensuring that I would never get out of credit card debt! With some effort, I improved my FICO credit score and my financial situation. Today my FICO Score 9 is 819, and I am very proud of that. If I did it, I know you can do even better with my FICO Score Improvement Journey as an encouragement.

Earlier in this book, I mentioned that one local bank denied me credit to fund my business. In August of 2018, that same bank offered me a $10,000 credit card with a 7% APR! When I saw the bank's invitation email, I thought I wouldn't take that credit card as retaliation for denying me a loan when I needed it most. But, then I asked myself, "What the hell do I have to lose?" I figured out the answer pretty quickly: "Nada! Nothing at all!"

Do you know the impact that credit card had on my credit rating? My credit rating changed from very good to excellent in eleven months! Wow!

This credit card has the best APR that I have ever had! That is not all, though. What is fascinating is that there are two credit cards that I have used for the last 13 years. For those 13 years, I called and called the big bank that owns the two credit cards requesting for an increase to my credit lines, but the bank insisted that I submit my latest pay stubs. I didn't know that the bank had been closely monitoring my credit reports such that, when my credit score skyrocketed and I got my fourth $10,000 credit card at a better APR, the big bank could not ignore me anymore! The bank increased my credit line on both of the credit cards by 79%!

On seeing my credit line make such an improvement, I asked myself some interesting questions:

Did the bank ask for my latest pay stub as it had done for all those years? No!

Did the bank ask for permission to increase my credit line?

Hell no!

Looking back at all the time my requests had been ignored, I thought, "I finally got some respect. Thanks be to my excellent FICO credit score!"

These days I frequently use one credit card that refunds 5% of most of my monthly purchases. I then clear my credit balance before the credit card company reports it to the credit rating bureaus. That arrangement ensures that the credit bureaus only get to know about the minimal or zero balance on my credit cards, which is usually less than 10% utilization. This has been one of my greatest secret weapons which has given a steady raise to my FICO credit score.

Summary: Pay your credit obligations on time even if it means paying the minimum.

Loans and credit card debt

This is the second most crucial factor in calculating Ken's FICO credit score. The total amount of money he owes in loans together with the amount he owes in credit card debt determine about 30% of his credit score. Here, institutions of lending pay particular interest to the ratio between outstanding and available credit card balances. If, for instance, Ken has $1,000 credit card debt and has only $1,000 available for use in his credit cards, his FICO credit score takes a hit. Ken will probably have a better FICO credit score if his credit card utilization is below 30%.

In his current 50% credit utilization, lenders might think he is in a "financial tight spot," even though in reality that might not be the case. The truth might be that Ken has simply been abroad on vacation and spent a little more money than planned due to a missed flight home. It also might be that Ken hopes to clear all his credit card debt in the next three months because he not only has a good job, but he is a great money manager. Since the credit rating bureaus might not use credit rating systems that take that into consideration, sudden and unusual available credit plunges on card balances could mean that Ken's credit rating takes a beating before it eventually recovers.

Total long-standing debts (e.g., college and mortgage debts) have a significant impact on Ken's credit rating, especially if he has substantial balances remaining from the original loans. Such loans also affect his credit rating because one's FICO credit score is the product of time. For long-standing debts like mortgages and college loans, please pay your dues on time. If you can pay these debts off, the better for you, but if you can't, don't sweat it. Keep doing what you need to do every month.

Summary: Avoid using more than 30% of available credit at all times.

Credit mix

The types of credit that Ken has determine about 10% of his credit score. Institutions of lending are interested in knowing how Ken manages different types of credit.

These types of credit include mortgages, car loans, college loans, and credit card debt. Without this credit mix, Ken is denied part or whole of this portion of the FICO credit score. If for example, Ken only has credit cards and absolutely no loan history, he might not enjoy the full 10% of this part of the FICO credit score.

I consider myself lucky in the credit mix area. A large portion of my college tuition loan is yet to be paid. Even though this weighs heavily on my pocket, I have a long-standing loan for lending institutions to see. This aspect of my borrowing history together with my credit card information gives lending institutions a long-term picture as to how I manage my money and credit resources.

At the back of my mind, I'm always thinking about how I will pay this college loan as fast as possible because I still owe $35,000, which is a substantial amount of money. Even though its APR is just 6%, compounded interest can add up quickly, and it could spell my financial doom. To achieve financial freedom, I plan to pay more than the minimum monthly payment. I advise my readers to follow a similar plan to pay off their long-standing debt to improve not only their FICO credit score but also their financial status.

Summary: Having some form of credit mix helps boost your credit score.

Credit history

The length of Ken's credit history is the third most important factor in determining Ken's FICO credit scores. It accounts for about 15% of his total FICO score. The longer your credit history, the better it is for you. If Ken has a 20-year credit history while his wife's spans five years, then Ken's FICO credit score will probably be better if we assume three things:

1. All other factors that determine FICO credit scores are the same for both of them.

2. All credit bureaus have the same information on file for both of them.

3. All the three credit rating bureaus, use the same algorithm/FICO score rating system for both of them.

Looking at Ken's 20-year credit history, lending institutions can predict how risky he might be when he borrows money. Of course, such institutions have to assume that his financial situation will remain as it has been.

As my college debt accumulated, I thought I could pay it off within three or four years after graduation because I was sure I was taking one of the most competitive degree courses, but today I still owe the government $35,000. From my assessment, my college debt obligation is probably a double-edged sword. On the one hand, for the past ten years that I have had this loan, one might look at it as a solid 10-year credit history, and on the other hand, one might say that I am saddled with a hard-to-pay loan that guarantees a never-ending financial pain. Like my credit card debt, it will also be gone because I'm working hard on it, and it will add to my portfolio of debts which I have paid successfully.

Apart from acquiring a costly second degree, which I now consider a credit/financial mistake, I also made other BIG stupid mistakes that ensured that my FICO credit score remained low for years.

About fourteen years ago, I canceled some credit cards simply because I thought that "if I did not use them, then I did not need them."

I relied heavily on cash and debit cards to make purchases and meet my debt obligations. Today, whenever possible and reasonable, I pay for my purchases and utilities with a credit card. Afterwards, I pay off the credit card balance before the end of the month.

I withdrew cash advances from two of my credit cards. I think that was the most credit/financially stupid thing that I have ever done. Cash advances are costly because you have to pay a cash advance fee, which is usually a percentage of the amount withdrawn. You also have to pay an interest fee, which is compounded every day until you pay back the borrowed cash. In my case, the interest rate was 26%. The sad thing about the $400 advanced to me was that I was not able to pay it back for a long time. That cash advance was one of the contributing factors that ruined my FICO score.

Listen to me, readers: I know that cash advances are tempting, but I want to urge you not to take that route unless you have an emergency.

It is essential for people with poor FICO scores or those who are beginning to build their credit history to read this book and consult with their family or friends who have longer credit histories so that unnecessary and expensive mistakes like mine are never repeated.

Summary: Remember that your credit history makes an essential portion of your FICO credit score, and do not cancel credit cards or credit accounts even if you may not need them. The time you have operated those credit cards or accounts paints a vital risk image about you to lending institutions.

New lines of credit

Every time Ken opens a new credit line, the financial institution that extends credit to him reports that information to credit reporting agencies. When that happens, his FICO credit score takes some beating in the short term. My guess is that when new line of credit information appears on Ken's credit reports, credit rating institutions wonder if Ken is having financial problems. Ken's FICO credit score only starts to improve after credit rating bureaus realize that he not only has more credit purchasing power to his name, but he also manages his credit resources well. A new line of credit has an impact on about 10% of Ken's total FICO credit score. That means that after Ken proves he can effectively manage his more robust credit resources, he might realize a 10% FICO credit score bump.

Earlier in this book, I mentioned my new $10,000 credit card. This credit card has had a remarkable effect on my FICO credit score. It was like a shot of adrenaline! At this juncture, I have to add that an improved FICO score has improved my life on multiple fronts because it saves me money.

Summary: In the short run, a new credit card might lower your FICO credit score, but that new credit has the potential to boost your FICO credit score in the long term.

14··Other Advantages of Having an Excellent FICO Credit Score

Periodic interest-free credit offers

Banks, like all other businesses, compete with each other for the same customers. To lure customers from their rivals, banks sometimes offer customers interest-free credit cards for a specified period. Look for such deals whenever you need to refinance your credit card debt.

In August 2017, I bought a $2,000 couch from a furniture store, and I used two of my credit cards, which had 23% APR. Not long after, I applied for a new credit card and got approved for $1,500. The surprising thing was that the credit card company allowed me to pay off my credit balances or make big purchases at 0% APR for a year. Who among you readers can say no to interest-free money when you have debts to pay? Certainly not me. Instantly, I paid off the remaining couch balance. That little effort saved me hundreds of dollars in interest fees and improved my FICO credit score.

Low-interest rate credit card offers

When you improve your credit score, lending institutions will be watching you. They know that with your improved credit score, their risk of doing business with you is lower. That is excellent news for them. They will, therefore, try to lure you into being their customer with low-interest credit cards. That is how I ended up with the $1,500 and $10,000 credit cards that I used to my advantage.

Credit cards that offer you cash back

If you buy stuff worth a lot of money every month and you have a high/excellent FICO score, then lending institutions most likely already know about you. Their creative managers try to figure out ways to get some of that money into their cash registers. Cash back for your purchases is almost a sure way to snag you.

A bank recently invited me to apply for an extraordinary credit card. I have to confess that for a long time, I have been green with envy for this card. The card offers 4% cash back for the first $7,000 you spend on gas each year. My family spends about $100 every week on gas, which makes this credit card a great way to save money, but I do not want to rock my boat because I have an eleven-month-old credit card. I know that hard inquiries take about two years to disappear from my credit report.

Other perks

I have also received an exciting offer to view/buy new two- and three-bedroom condos in a nearby city. I might go and see them even though at the moment, I do not think it is wise to buy a house at the current inflated prices.

New houses have been built right and left in the city where I have lived for almost twenty years, but never before have I been invited to view any property by anyone. Not even a doghouse!

I interpret these offers to mean that great/excellent FICO scores allow us to get the best deals from those that we transact business with — banks, auto-dealers, and insurance firms.

Notes

Notes